50 Premium Yogurt and Ice Cream Dishes

By: Kelly Johnson

Table of Contents

- Pistachio Gelato with Candied Orange Peel
- Greek Yogurt Parfait with Honey and Walnuts
- Matcha Ice Cream with Red Bean Paste
- Rosewater and Saffron Frozen Yogurt
- Salted Caramel Ice Cream with Pretzel Crumble
- Mango Lassi Frozen Yogurt
- Bourbon Vanilla Bean Ice Cream
- Coconut Yogurt with Pineapple and Toasted Coconut
- Black Sesame Ice Cream
- Lemon Yogurt Tart with Berry Compote
- Earl Grey Ice Cream with Lavender Honey
- Chocolate Swirl Frozen Yogurt
- Strawberry Basil Ice Cream
- Yogurt and Honey Mousse
- Espresso Ice Cream with Chocolate Shards
- Spiced Pumpkin Frozen Yogurt
- Blueberry Cheesecake Ice Cream
- Chai Spiced Frozen Yogurt
- Raspberry Ripple Ice Cream
- Greek Yogurt Cheesecake
- Tiramisu Gelato
- Pomegranate Yogurt Sorbet
- White Chocolate Ice Cream with Raspberries
- Fig and Honey Yogurt Bowl
- Matcha Frozen Yogurt with Mochi
- Peanut Butter Ice Cream with Chocolate Chunks
- Yogurt and Granola Popsicles
- Roasted Banana Ice Cream
- Yogurt Panna Cotta with Mixed Berries
- Maple Walnut Ice Cream
- Tropical Yogurt Bowl with Dragon Fruit
- Blackberry Sorbet with Greek Yogurt
- Cinnamon Ice Cream with Apple Compote
- Tahini Yogurt Parfait with Dates
- Mint Chocolate Chip Ice Cream

- Blood Orange Frozen Yogurt
- Spicy Chocolate Ice Cream with Cayenne
- Yogurt Bark with Nuts and Dried Fruit
- Avocado Ice Cream with Lime
- Cardamom Frozen Yogurt
- Dark Chocolate and Sea Salt Gelato
- Lemon Curd Frozen Yogurt
- Rhubarb and Strawberry Yogurt Bowl
- Mascarpone Ice Cream with Fig Jam
- Almond Yogurt with Cherry Compote
- Watermelon Sorbet with Yogurt Swirl
- Black Forest Ice Cream
- Honey Lavender Frozen Yogurt
- Pear and Ginger Yogurt Bowl
- Coconut Ice Cream with Mango Salsa

Pistachio Gelato with Candied Orange Peel

Ingredients

For the Gelato:

- 2 cups whole milk
- 1 cup heavy cream
- 4 large egg yolks
- 2/3 cup sugar
- 1 cup unsalted pistachios
- 1/2 tsp vanilla extract
- Pinch of salt

For the Candied Orange Peel:

- 2 orange peels, sliced
- 1 cup sugar
- 1/2 cup water

Instructions

1. **Candied Orange Peel:** Blanch orange peel in boiling water three times. Simmer in sugar and water for 30 minutes until translucent. Let dry, then chop.
2. **Pistachio Gelato Base:** Grind pistachios into a paste. Heat milk and cream until steaming. Whisk yolks, sugar, and salt, then temper with hot milk. Return to the pot and cook until slightly thickened. Stir in pistachio paste and vanilla. Strain, cool, and chill.
3. **Churn:** Churn in an ice cream maker. Add candied orange peel in the last 5 minutes. Freeze until firm.

Greek Yogurt Parfait with Honey and Walnuts

Ingredients:

- 2 cups Greek yogurt
- 1/4 cup honey
- 1/3 cup walnuts, chopped and toasted
- Fresh fruit (optional)

Instructions:

1. Layer Greek yogurt, honey, and walnuts in a glass.
2. Repeat layers for a parfait effect.
3. Top with fresh fruit if desired. Serve immediately.

Matcha Ice Cream with Red Bean Paste

Ingredients:

- 2 cups whole milk
- 1 cup heavy cream
- 4 egg yolks
- 2/3 cup sugar
- 2 tbsp matcha powder
- 1/2 cup sweetened red bean paste

Instructions:

1. Whisk egg yolks and sugar until pale. Heat milk and cream; temper into egg mixture.
2. Dissolve matcha powder into the mixture. Chill, then churn in an ice cream maker.
3. Fold in red bean paste before freezing. Serve cold.

Rosewater and Saffron Frozen Yogurt

Ingredients:

- 2 cups plain Greek yogurt
- 1/2 cup sugar
- 1 tbsp rosewater
- A pinch of saffron threads

Instructions:

1. Dissolve sugar and saffron in 1 tbsp warm water. Combine with yogurt and rosewater.
2. Chill and churn in an ice cream maker. Freeze until firm.

Salted Caramel Ice Cream with Pretzel Crumble

Ingredients:

- 1 cup sugar
- 2 cups heavy cream
- 1 cup whole milk
- 4 egg yolks
- 1/2 tsp sea salt
- 1/2 cup crushed pretzels

Instructions:

1. Cook sugar until caramelized, then whisk in cream and milk.
2. Temper yolks with the hot mixture, cook until thickened, and add salt. Chill and churn in an ice cream maker.
3. Layer with pretzel crumble before freezing.

Mango Lassi Frozen Yogurt

Ingredients:

- 2 cups plain Greek yogurt
- 1 cup mango purée
- 1/4 cup sugar
- 1/2 tsp cardamom powder

Instructions:

1. Blend yogurt, mango purée, sugar, and cardamom.
2. Chill the mixture and churn in an ice cream maker. Freeze until set.

Bourbon Vanilla Bean Ice Cream

Ingredients:

- 2 cups heavy cream
- 1 cup whole milk
- 4 egg yolks
- 2/3 cup sugar
- 1 vanilla bean, split and scraped
- 2 tbsp bourbon

Instructions:

1. Heat cream, milk, and vanilla. Temper yolks with sugar and the hot mixture, cook until thickened.
2. Stir in bourbon, chill, and churn in an ice cream maker. Freeze.

Coconut Yogurt with Pineapple and Toasted Coconut

Ingredients:

- 2 cups coconut yogurt
- 1 cup fresh pineapple chunks
- 1/4 cup toasted coconut flakes
- 2 tbsp honey

Instructions:

1. Layer coconut yogurt, pineapple, and toasted coconut in bowls.
2. Drizzle with honey and serve.

Black Sesame Ice Cream

Ingredients:

- 1 cup heavy cream
- 1 cup whole milk
- 4 egg yolks
- 2/3 cup sugar
- 1/4 cup black sesame paste

Instructions:

1. Heat cream and milk. Whisk yolks and sugar, temper with hot liquid, and cook until thickened.
2. Stir in sesame paste, chill, and churn in an ice cream maker. Freeze until firm.

Lemon Yogurt Tart with Berry Compote

Ingredients:

- 1 pre-baked tart crust
- 1 cup Greek yogurt
- 1/4 cup lemon juice
- 1/4 cup sugar
- 2 cups mixed berries
- 2 tbsp sugar (for compote)

Instructions:

1. Whisk yogurt, lemon juice, and sugar; pour into the crust. Chill until set.
2. Simmer berries and sugar for compote; cool and spoon over tart before serving.

Earl Grey Ice Cream with Lavender Honey

Ingredients:

- 2 cups heavy cream
- 1 cup whole milk
- 4 egg yolks
- 2/3 cup sugar
- 3 Earl Grey tea bags
- 2 tbsp lavender honey

Instructions:

1. Infuse cream and milk with tea bags; strain. Temper egg yolks with sugar and the mixture; cook until thickened.
2. Chill, churn in an ice cream maker, and drizzle with lavender honey when serving.

Chocolate Swirl Frozen Yogurt

Ingredients:

- 2 cups plain Greek yogurt
- 1/2 cup sugar
- 1/4 cup melted dark chocolate

Instructions:

1. Mix yogurt and sugar; churn in an ice cream maker.
2. Swirl in melted chocolate before freezing.

Strawberry Basil Ice Cream

Ingredients:

- 2 cups fresh strawberries, puréed
- 2 cups heavy cream
- 1 cup whole milk
- 1/2 cup sugar
- 2 tbsp chopped basil

Instructions:

1. Blend cream, milk, sugar, strawberries, and basil. Chill and churn in an ice cream maker.

Yogurt and Honey Mousse

Ingredients:

- 1 cup Greek yogurt
- 1/2 cup heavy cream, whipped
- 1/4 cup honey
- 1 tsp vanilla extract

Instructions:

1. Fold whipped cream into yogurt, add honey and vanilla. Chill before serving.

Espresso Ice Cream with Chocolate Shards

Ingredients:

- 2 cups heavy cream
- 1 cup whole milk
- 4 egg yolks
- 1/2 cup sugar
- 2 tbsp espresso powder
- 1/3 cup dark chocolate, chopped

Instructions:

1. Dissolve espresso in warm cream and milk; temper egg yolks and sugar. Cook until thickened, chill, churn, and fold in chocolate shards.

Spiced Pumpkin Frozen Yogurt

Ingredients:

- 1 cup pumpkin purée
- 2 cups plain Greek yogurt
- 1/3 cup brown sugar
- 1 tsp pumpkin spice

Instructions:

1. Mix all ingredients, chill, churn in an ice cream maker, and freeze.

Blueberry Cheesecake Ice Cream

Ingredients:

- 1 cup cream cheese, softened
- 2 cups heavy cream
- 1 cup whole milk
- 1/2 cup sugar
- 1/2 cup blueberry compote

Instructions:

1. Blend cream cheese, cream, milk, and sugar. Chill, churn in an ice cream maker, and swirl in blueberry compote before freezing.

Chai Spiced Frozen Yogurt

Ingredients:

- 2 cups plain Greek yogurt
- 1/2 cup sugar
- 1 tsp chai spice mix

Instructions:

1. Mix yogurt, sugar, and chai spices. Chill, churn in an ice cream maker, and freeze.

Raspberry Ripple Ice Cream

Ingredients:

- 2 cups heavy cream
- 1 cup whole milk
- 4 egg yolks
- 2/3 cup sugar
- 1 cup raspberry purée

Instructions:

1. Heat cream and milk. Whisk egg yolks and sugar, then temper with the hot mixture. Cook until thickened.
2. Chill, churn in an ice cream maker, and swirl in raspberry purée before freezing.

Greek Yogurt Cheesecake

Ingredients:

- 2 cups Greek yogurt
- 1 cup cream cheese, softened
- 1/2 cup sugar
- 1/4 cup lemon juice
- 1 pre-baked graham cracker crust

Instructions:

1. Blend Greek yogurt, cream cheese, sugar, and lemon juice.
2. Pour into the crust and chill until set.

Tiramisu Gelato

Ingredients:

- 2 cups heavy cream
- 1 cup whole milk
- 4 egg yolks
- 2/3 cup sugar
- 2 tbsp coffee liqueur
- 1 tsp vanilla extract
- 1/2 cup mascarpone cheese

Instructions:

1. Heat cream and milk. Whisk yolks and sugar, then temper with hot mixture. Cook until thickened.
2. Stir in coffee liqueur, vanilla, and mascarpone. Chill, churn, and freeze.

Pomegranate Yogurt Sorbet

Ingredients:

- 2 cups pomegranate juice
- 1 cup Greek yogurt
- 1/2 cup sugar

Instructions:

1. Mix pomegranate juice, yogurt, and sugar.
2. Chill and churn in an ice cream maker. Freeze until set.

White Chocolate Ice Cream with Raspberries

Ingredients:

- 2 cups heavy cream
- 1 cup whole milk
- 4 egg yolks
- 2/3 cup sugar
- 1/2 cup white chocolate, melted
- 1/2 cup fresh raspberries

Instructions:

1. Heat cream and milk. Whisk egg yolks and sugar, then temper with the hot mixture. Cook until thickened.
2. Stir in melted white chocolate, chill, churn, and fold in raspberries before freezing.

Fig and Honey Yogurt Bowl

Ingredients:

- 2 cups Greek yogurt
- 1/4 cup honey
- 6 fresh figs, sliced

Instructions:

1. Spoon yogurt into bowls, drizzle with honey, and top with sliced figs. Serve immediately.

Matcha Frozen Yogurt with Mochi

Ingredients:

- 2 cups plain Greek yogurt
- 1/4 cup sugar
- 2 tbsp matcha powder
- 1/2 cup mochi, chopped

Instructions:

1. Whisk yogurt, sugar, and matcha powder.
2. Chill, churn in an ice cream maker, and fold in chopped mochi before freezing.

Peanut Butter Ice Cream with Chocolate Chunks

Ingredients:

- 2 cups heavy cream
- 1 cup whole milk
- 4 egg yolks
- 2/3 cup sugar
- 1/2 cup peanut butter
- 1/3 cup dark chocolate chunks

Instructions:

1. Heat cream and milk. Whisk egg yolks and sugar, then temper with the hot mixture. Cook until thickened.
2. Stir in peanut butter, chill, churn, and fold in chocolate chunks before freezing.

Yogurt and Granola Popsicles

Ingredients:

- 2 cups Greek yogurt
- 1/4 cup honey
- 1/2 cup granola

Instructions:

1. Mix Greek yogurt and honey.
2. Layer yogurt and granola in popsicle molds, freeze until solid.

Roasted Banana Ice Cream

Ingredients:

- 4 ripe bananas, sliced
- 2 cups heavy cream
- 1 cup whole milk
- 1/2 cup sugar

Instructions:

1. Roast bananas at 375°F for 15-20 minutes.
2. Blend roasted bananas with cream, milk, and sugar. Chill, churn, and freeze.

Yogurt Panna Cotta with Mixed Berries

Ingredients:

- 2 cups Greek yogurt
- 1 cup heavy cream
- 1/4 cup sugar
- 1 tsp vanilla extract
- 1 tbsp gelatin
- 2 cups mixed berries

Instructions:

1. Dissolve gelatin in warm water, then mix with yogurt, cream, sugar, and vanilla.
2. Pour into molds and chill until set. Top with mixed berries before serving.

Maple Walnut Ice Cream

Ingredients:

- 2 cups heavy cream
- 1 cup whole milk
- 4 egg yolks
- 2/3 cup maple syrup
- 1/2 cup chopped walnuts

Instructions:

1. Heat cream and milk. Whisk yolks and syrup, temper with hot mixture, and cook until thickened.
2. Chill, churn, and fold in walnuts before freezing.

Tropical Yogurt Bowl with Dragon Fruit

Ingredients:

- 2 cups Greek yogurt
- 1/2 cup pineapple chunks
- 1/2 cup mango chunks
- 1 dragon fruit, sliced

Instructions:

1. Layer yogurt with tropical fruits in a bowl. Top with sliced dragon fruit and serve.

Blackberry Sorbet with Greek Yogurt

Ingredients:

- 2 cups blackberries
- 1 cup Greek yogurt
- 1/2 cup sugar

Instructions:

1. Blend blackberries, yogurt, and sugar.
2. Chill and churn in an ice cream maker, then freeze until firm.

Cinnamon Ice Cream with Apple Compote

Ingredients:

- 2 cups heavy cream
- 1 cup whole milk
- 4 egg yolks
- 2/3 cup sugar
- 1 tsp ground cinnamon
- 2 apples, peeled and chopped
- 1/4 cup brown sugar

Instructions:

1. Heat cream, milk, cinnamon, and sugar. Whisk yolks and temper with the hot mixture, cooking until thickened.
2. Cook apples with brown sugar into compote. Chill, churn the ice cream, and serve with apple compote.

Tahini Yogurt Parfait with Dates

Ingredients:

- 2 cups Greek yogurt
- 1/4 cup tahini
- 1/4 cup honey
- 6 dates, chopped

Instructions:

1. Mix yogurt, tahini, and honey.
2. Layer with chopped dates in a parfait glass and serve.

Mint Chocolate Chip Ice Cream

Ingredients:

- 2 cups heavy cream
- 1 cup whole milk
- 4 egg yolks
- 2/3 cup sugar
- 1 tsp peppermint extract
- 1/2 cup chocolate chips

Instructions:

1. Heat cream and milk. Whisk yolks and sugar, temper with hot mixture, and cook until thickened.
2. Stir in peppermint extract, chill, churn, and fold in chocolate chips before freezing.

Blood Orange Frozen Yogurt

Ingredients:

- 2 cups Greek yogurt
- 1/2 cup blood orange juice
- 1/4 cup honey

Instructions:

1. Whisk yogurt, blood orange juice, and honey together.
2. Chill, churn in an ice cream maker, and freeze until set.

Spicy Chocolate Ice Cream with Cayenne

Ingredients:

- 2 cups heavy cream
- 1 cup whole milk
- 4 egg yolks
- 2/3 cup sugar
- 1/2 cup cocoa powder
- 1/4 tsp cayenne pepper

Instructions:

1. Heat cream and milk. Whisk yolks and sugar, temper with hot mixture, and cook until thickened.
2. Stir in cocoa powder and cayenne, chill, churn, and freeze.

Yogurt Bark with Nuts and Dried Fruit

Ingredients:

- 2 cups Greek yogurt
- 1/4 cup honey
- 1/2 cup mixed nuts, chopped
- 1/2 cup dried fruit, chopped

Instructions:

1. Mix yogurt and honey.
2. Spread on a baking sheet, top with nuts and dried fruit, and freeze until solid. Break into pieces.

Avocado Ice Cream with Lime

Ingredients:

- 2 ripe avocados
- 2 cups heavy cream
- 1 cup whole milk
- 1/2 cup sugar
- 2 tbsp lime juice

Instructions:

1. Blend avocado, cream, milk, sugar, and lime juice until smooth.
2. Chill, churn in an ice cream maker, and freeze.

Cardamom Frozen Yogurt

Ingredients:

- 2 cups Greek yogurt
- 1/4 cup sugar
- 1 tsp ground cardamom

Instructions:

1. Mix yogurt, sugar, and cardamom.
2. Chill, churn in an ice cream maker, and freeze until firm.

Dark Chocolate and Sea Salt Gelato

Ingredients:

- 2 cups heavy cream
- 1 cup whole milk
- 4 egg yolks
- 2/3 cup sugar
- 1/2 cup dark chocolate, melted
- 1/4 tsp sea salt

Instructions:

1. Heat cream and milk. Whisk yolks and sugar, temper with hot mixture, and cook until thickened.
2. Stir in melted chocolate and sea salt, chill, churn, and freeze.

Lemon Curd Frozen Yogurt

Ingredients:

- 2 cups Greek yogurt
- 1/2 cup lemon curd
- 1/4 cup honey

Instructions:

1. Mix yogurt, lemon curd, and honey.
2. Chill, churn in an ice cream maker, and freeze until set.

Rhubarb and Strawberry Yogurt Bowl

Ingredients:

- 2 cups Greek yogurt
- 1/2 cup rhubarb compote
- 1/2 cup strawberries, sliced
- 1 tbsp honey

Instructions:

1. Spoon yogurt into bowls. Top with rhubarb compote, strawberries, and honey. Serve immediately.

Mascarpone Ice Cream with Fig Jam

Ingredients:

- 2 cups heavy cream
- 1 cup whole milk
- 4 egg yolks
- 2/3 cup sugar
- 1/2 cup mascarpone cheese
- 1/2 cup fig jam

Instructions:

1. Heat cream and milk. Whisk yolks and sugar, temper with hot mixture, and cook until thickened.
2. Stir in mascarpone cheese, chill, churn, and swirl in fig jam before freezing.

Almond Yogurt with Cherry Compote

Ingredients:

- 2 cups Greek yogurt
- 1/4 cup almond butter
- 1/4 cup honey
- 1 cup cherries, pitted and chopped
- 1 tbsp sugar

Instructions:

1. Mix yogurt, almond butter, and honey.
2. Cook cherries with sugar into compote. Top yogurt with cherry compote and serve.

Watermelon Sorbet with Yogurt Swirl

Ingredients:

- 2 cups watermelon, blended into puree
- 1/2 cup sugar
- 1 cup Greek yogurt

Instructions:

1. Mix watermelon puree and sugar, then churn in an ice cream maker.
2. Swirl in yogurt before freezing.

Black Forest Ice Cream

Ingredients:

- 2 cups heavy cream
- 1 cup whole milk
- 4 egg yolks
- 2/3 cup sugar
- 1/2 cup chocolate syrup
- 1/2 cup cherries, chopped

Instructions:

1. Heat cream and milk. Whisk yolks and sugar, temper with hot mixture, and cook until thickened.
2. Stir in chocolate syrup, chill, churn, and fold in cherries before freezing.

Honey Lavender Frozen Yogurt

Ingredients:

- 2 cups Greek yogurt
- 1/4 cup honey
- 1 tbsp dried lavender

Instructions:

1. Infuse honey with lavender by heating gently, then strain.
2. Mix honey with yogurt, chill, churn in an ice cream maker, and freeze until set.

Pear and Ginger Yogurt Bowl

Ingredients:

- 2 cups Greek yogurt
- 1 pear, chopped
- 1/4 tsp ground ginger
- 1 tbsp honey

Instructions:

1. Mix yogurt with ground ginger and honey.
2. Top with fresh pear and serve immediately.

Coconut Ice Cream with Mango Salsa

Ingredients:

- 2 cups coconut milk
- 1 cup heavy cream
- 2/3 cup sugar
- 1 mango, diced
- 1 tbsp lime juice

Instructions:

1. Heat coconut milk and cream. Whisk sugar, then temper with hot mixture and cook until thickened.
2. Chill, churn, and serve with fresh mango salsa (mango and lime).

www.ingramcontent.com/pod-product-compliance
Lightning Source LLC
LaVergne TN
LVHW081501060526
838201LV00056BA/2875